Faster, Faster! Nice and Slow!

For Nick H. – S.H.
For Leo – N.S.

PUFFIN BOOKS

Published by the Penguin Group: London, New York, Australia, Canada, India, Ireland, New Zealand and South Africa
Penguin Books Ltd, Registered Offices: 80 Strand, London WC2R 0RL, England

puffinbooks.com

First published 2005
Published in this edition 2006

010 - 10

Text and illustrations copyright © Sue Heap and Nick Sharratt, 2005

ISBN: 978-0-140-56787-8

Faster, Faster! Nice and Slow!

Sue Heap and **Nick Sharratt**

PUFFIN

We're Nick and Sue,

Hello, hello!

We're up above,

We're down below!

A quiet cat,

This road's bumpy,

This road's flat!

W're so h avy,

We're so light,

I hold on tight!

This bird is **big**,

This bird is small,

A lot of clothes,

No clothes at all!

I'm near to you,

I'm far away,

It's very cold,

It's hot today.

In we
come

and out
we go,

Faster, faster!

Nice and *s l o w*.

I'm getting wet,

I'm warm and dry,

Goodbye, goodbye!

Goodbye, Nick!
Goodbye, Sue!